Contents

INTRODUCTION

1 Budgies enjoy human company

They can be great fun to keep, and require only simple and inexpensive care. It is not surprising that this friendly, playful and colourful mini-parrot has become the most popular pet bird in the world. However, like all pets, budgies need time and commitment. They need company, daily exercise outside the cage, and protection from cats, fumes and possible escape routes. One word of warning...

...they can be messy (you cannot house-train a budgie!) and they can be noisy. Before you buy a budgie, be sure you are ready to take on the responsibility.

Above: The budgerigar is the most widely kept pet bird in the world.

2 Budgies belong to the parrot family

In their native Australia, they live in huge flocks, which may be thousands of birds strong. Their natural habitat is dry grassland, and in times of drought they have to fly hundreds of miles in quest of food and water. Wild budgerigars are smaller than their domesticated cousins, and retain the original colour scheme of light green plumage with yellow heads and black-banded back and wings. The name 'Budgerigar' comes from a native Aboriginal word Betcherrygah meaning 'good eating', but today we know them better as good pets.

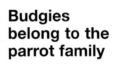

GOLD MEDAL GUIDE

Golden tips for keeping your first

BUDGIE

AMANDA O'NEILL

Interpet Publishing

Editor: Philip de Ste. Croix

Designer: Phil Clucas MSIAD

Studio photography:
Neil Sutherland

Production management:
Consortium, Poslingford, Suffolk

Print production:
Sino Publishing House Ltd.,
Hong Kong

Printed and bound
in the Far East

Published by Interpet Publishing, Vincent Lane, Dorking
Surrey RH4 3YX, England

© 2004 Interpet Publishing Ltd.
All rights reserved   ISBN 1-84286-094-1

The Author   Amanda O'Neill was
born in Sussex in 1951 and educated
at the University of Exeter, where she
read medieval literature. She has never
lived without a variety of pets, ranging
from rabbits and gerbils to giant snails
and hissing cockroaches. Currently she
lives in the Midlands with her husband
and son, along with five dogs, a
cat, Roborowski hamsters
and a collection of
coldwater fish.

*The recommendations in this book
are given without any guarantees on the part
of the author and publisher. If in doubt, seek
the advice of a vet or pet-care specialist.*

Above: Wild budgies are very much flock birds.

3

The first budgies arrived in Europe in 1840

Here they first bred successfully in the 1850s, but it was the development of colour mutations that inspired the budgerigar craze. The first recorded mutation, yellow, occurred in 1870, followed a few years later by blue. By the 1920s budgies came in a range of colours, fetching astronomical prices. A decade later prices dropped and brightly coloured budgies became widely available as pets. Today the budgie occurs in more colour varieties than most other species. English and American types differ, English breeders having developed a larger, more vibrantly coloured exhibition bird.

GOLD MEDAL TIPS

ASTHMA WARNING

Budgies may be unsuitable pets for anyone with asthma, as they shed feather dust – not as much as parrots, but enough to cause a problem. If anyone in your family suffers from allergies, it is advisable to check with your doctor before introducing a bird into the household.

LONG LIFESPAN

Budgies are not a short term commitment. The average lifespan is eight to ten years, but 14 years is not unusual. Budgies become attached to their owners, and do not change homes happily, so think about the future before buying a bird.

YOUNG CHILDREN

Budgies are not recommended as pets for children under eight years old. Very young children are unlikely to appreciate a pet that they cannot hug and hold, and small birds are easily injured. Older children who can understand the bird's needs can enjoy a relationship with a budgie.

FEATHER DUSTERS
Budgies with abnormally long, soft feathers like a Silky bantam occasionally occur and are known as feather dusters or chrysanthemums.
Unlike Silky bantams, these are not a true-breeding variety but defective specimens. They have health problems, cannot fly and rarely live very long.

MIX 'N' MATCH
Often, more than one variant is combined in the same bird. For example, an opaline cinnamon dark blue is a bird with dark blue ground colour and brown (cinnamon) markings which end at the top of the wings (the opaline pattern). Variety names can end up being quite lengthy!

WEIRD WINGS
Considerable variety in wing markings has developed. Spangles have their wing markings in reverse, with a dark edge to each feather, while clearwings have no wing markings at all, just pale wings (usually white or yellow) contrasting with a darker body colour.

4 VARIETIES

Four basic colours – but many shades

There are no blacks, browns, reds or pinks to be found among budgies, just four basic colours: green, yellow, blue and white. However, these extend over a wide range of light, dark and medium shades, and come in various combinations. Budgies whose colour pattern follows the wild type (with black wing markings and cheek spots) are known as normals. They come in greens (light, dark and olive), blues (sky blue, cobalt, mauve and violet) and greys. Normal light green and sky blue are the commonest varieties among pet budgies.

Left: Blues come in a variety of shades from soft pastel to bright.

Right: Colour variations from the original green sometimes occur in the wild, but have never spread. Standing out from the crowd attracts predators! It took years of work by dedicated budgie breeders to produce the incredible spectrum of colours we enjoy today.

A choice of patterns

The normal varieties have black barring on the wings and back of the head and black cheek spots. In other varieties, these markings may be brown (cinnamon), grey (greywing), very pale (whitewing), or softly mottled (spangle). There are also opalines with reduced markings at the top of the wings and back of head, albinos (white) and lutinos (yellow) with no markings at all, pieds with variegated or banded markings, and even 'rainbows', combining green, yellow and blue together. All varieties are equally hardy and lovable.

Left: Colours include grey, lutino (yellow), blue, green and assorted combinations of these. What other bird offers so much choice?

Crests and tufts

Apart from colour, there is only one successful variation on the basic budgie model: the crested. It occurs in three forms: full-crested (or full-circular crest), with a cap of floppy feathers on top of the head, half-crested (or half-circular crest), with a smaller cap covering only part of the head, and tufted, with just a little upright crest at the front of the head. A much less common variant is the long-flighted budgie, with flight feathers so elongated as to hinder flying, a handicap which means it has never become popular.

Right: Deformed feathers form a 'feather duster'.

CHOOSING A BUDGIE

Where to buy

7

Most pet-shops stock a good selection of budgies, as well as cages, food, etc. Alternatively, breeders often advertise surplus stock for sale in local newspapers or on vets' notice-boards. Only buy from shops or breeders where the birds are well housed, well tended and tame, and where their attendants are knowledgeable about them and can answer questions. If you want a specific colour variety, you may have to seek a specialist cagebird publication to locate a breeder.

Above: Aviary-raised birds may not be hand-tame, but they should be accustomed to huma presence and not panic when you visit.

Crown
Cere
Nare
Beak
Nape
Mantel
Rump
Breast
Tail feathers
(retrices)

Right: A healthy bird looks spruce, smart and alert. In birds, scruffiness isn't cute – it's a sign of ill health.

Choosing a healthy bird

8

A healthy bird will look smart, with sleek plumage, bright eyes and an alert expression. Look for undamaged tail and wing feathers, clean feet with four norm toes, and a well-shaped beak. Above a a healthy bird should be active, lively an socializing with its cage-mates. Untid feathers, a dirty vent area, noisy breathing, or discharge from the ey or nostrils indicate problems, and healthy-looking birds which sha a cage with sick ones are also be avoided.

*ght: Male and
male budgies
ffer in the colour
the cere: blue
males, brown
females*

Female bird　　　*Male bird*

What age? Baby budgies are ready to
leave home at around six to nine weeks old,
and at this age they are easy to tame.
oungsters can be recognized by their pinkish cere
he waxy area around the nostrils) and the
attern of barring on the head, which continues
 the way down the forehead. At around
ree months of age, the forehead bars
egin to disappear, and the cere changes
olour (blue for males, brown for females).
rds older than three months will take
nger to settle in to a new home.

One bird
or two?

udgerigars need
ompany. You can
ave a closer relationship with one
udgie than with two, but this is only
r on the bird if you are at home
th him most of the day. Unless you
ave a lot of time for your budgie, two
rds will be much happier than one, and
ey will keep you entertained with their
ntics. Pick a male and female (they won't
eed unless you provide a nest-box) or two
ales: two females may squabble.

MALE OR FEMALE?
*Either sex makes an equally
satisfactory pet. The sexes can
be distinguished by the colour of
the cere, which is usually blue in
adult males, brown in adult
females. In a few varieties such
as albinos, lutinos and recessive
pieds, males have a flesh-
coloured cere.*

CHECK BEAKS
*Always check the beak of your
prospective purchase. The
upper bill should fit neatly over
the lower bill. If you buy a bird
with an undershot (lower bill
projecting over upper) or
crossed bill, it will have
difficulty feeding and you
will have long-term
care problems.*

TRANSPORT HOME
*The seller should
provide a cardboard
box with air holes.
The journey
home will be
stressful, so
make it as short
as possible.
Carry the box
in your hands,
protecting it
from jerks and
jolts. On a
cold day, wrap
your coat loosely
round it, keeping air
holes clear.*

*Left: For transport
home, a budgie is safer
in a small box than jolting
around in a full-size cage.*

HOUSING YOUR BIRD

11 The bigger the cage, the better

Budgies are active birds which need space to fly, climb and play. Many cages are small, cramped prisons, allowing the inmate to do little more than hop from perch to perch. The minimum size for a cage should be 50cm (20in) long, 30cm (12in) wide and 45cm (18in) high, and ideally larger. This makes a comfortable home. However, no matter how large the cage, your budgie needs daily flying time outside it to maintain his health.

Right: A 'starter kit' includes food and water containers, ladders, perches and toys as well as the cage itself.

12 The design of the cage is also important

Cage width matters more than height. Budgies fly horizontally, so a tall, narrow cage provides less usable space than a lower, wider one. The bars should be horizontal, not vertical, to allow your pet climbing exercise. Look for bars that are no wider apart than 12mm (0.5in), so that the budgie cannot trap his head between them. A well-designed cage should also be easy to clean, with a sliding tray in the base to make daily floor-cleaning a simple task.

13

Choose the cage site carefully

Pick a room where your budgie can enjoy plenty of company, but not constant noisy activity – and not the kitchen, where cooking fumes and temperature changes will affect the bird. Make sure the cage is not in direct sunlight or draughts. A position directly in front of a window is unsuitable as it will be too hot in summer, and too cold in winter. Standing the cage in a corner will protect it from being bumped or knocked over.

Right: An outdoor aviary must include a weather-proof shelter.

A cage is not enough

14

Budgies need access to exercise space. Birds kept in an outside aviary can enjoy plenty of free-flying exercise, but will not become so tame.

For birds kept indoors, you can build an indoor aviary (a flight), but not everybody has space for this. It is quite sufficient to keep your bird in a suitable cage, but let him out daily for a couple of hours to explore the room. When siting the cage, it makes sense therefore to pick the room most suitable for a free-flying budgie (see pages 20-21).

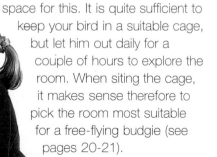

Left: Cage design should satisfy the bird's need for space, and the owner's need for easy cleaning facilities.

GOLD MEDAL TIPS

CUTTLEFISH BONE

All budgies should have a piece of cuttlefish bone (available from pet-shops) clipped to the cage wire. Nibbling on this provides the bird with essential minerals, helps to keep its beak in good trim, and also provides hours of amusement. Budgies need to chew!

Above: Cuttlefish bones provide calcium as well as beak exercise.

TEMPTING TOYS

Budgies enjoy toys to play with, and a wide variety of swings, ladders, balls, mirrors and clip-on plastic birds can be found in pet-shops. Avoid metal or breakable toys, and don't over-clutter the cage. Offering a different toy each day will keep your budgie's interest alive.

CLIMBING IS GOOD

Climbing, using feet and beak, is fun and good exercise for a budgie. Inside his cage, he can scramble up the bars, and he will also enjoy a ladder. For exercise outside the cage, try setting up a climbing tree, wedging a sturdy branch firmly into a soil-filled bucket.

Perches are not just for sitting on

15

Suitable perches are vital to maintain healthy feet. Budgies need a choice of perches of varying widths, say 12-20mm (0.5-0.75in). If all perches are the same size, under-exercised foot muscles will lead to sore or deformed feet. Clean branch from fruit trees offer more variety of grip than dowelling. Place perch as far apart as possible, and never situate one directly above another, to avoid fouling. Chewed perche will need replacing from time to time.

Left: Pet-shops stock a wide range of plastic or dowelling perches.

Floor covering

16

Seed husks and droppings soon fo a cage floor, so you need a disposa floor covering. Sand or gravel is ide sand sheets, available from stores, make cleaning ea as they can be simply replaced each day. Some cages have a metal grill above a bottom tray, allowing waste to fall through This protects the bir from their droppings but deprives them c the fun of pecking about on the cage fl

Sand sheets fit inside a pull-out tray

FURNISHING THE CAGE

Above: A hooded, clip-on food bowl keeps food clean as well as accessible.

17 Food and water containers

Food and water need to be protected from fouling, so open containers are unsuitable. Choose food and water bowls which clip to the cage wire and are fitted with plastic shields to keep the contents clean, and never position these directly under perches. For water, a gravity-fed drinking bottle clipped to the bars is better than a bowl to keep the water unsoiled. Make sure the spout is of strong metal, to stand up to chewing.

18 A bath is an essential, not a luxury

Regular bathing keeps feathers clean and healthy, as well as providing amusement. You can simply provide a saucer of tepid water placed on the cage floor, removing it immediately after use. However, a purpose-made plastic bath-house designed to hang in the cage door opening is less messy. Choose one with a grooved floor to provide a grip for your bird's feet. Not all budgies enjoy a bath; those which don't will benefit from an occasional spray from an atomiser.

Right: A clip-on bath-house attached to the cage doorway prevents mess, and is easy to fit and to remove.

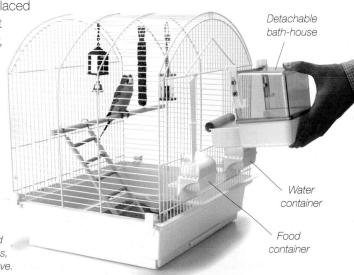

Detachable bath-house

Water container

Food container

FOOD AND FEEDING

19

Mixed seeds form the basis of budgie diet

Various seed mixes designed for budgies are readily available from pet-shops. These should include canary seed, millet, red rape, linseed and niger. Some seed mixes also contain vitamin and mineral supplements in pellet form. Budgies will nibble off the husk of the seeds, eating only the kernel, and it is essential to clear the left-over husks each day to prevent them from covering the remaining food – budgies won't hunt under the husks for their dinner. Buy food in small quantities as it will go off if stored for long periods.

Carrot

Broccoli

Seed mix

Spinach

Dri-greens

Chickweed

Apple

20 Green food and fruit are important too

Supplement the seed mix with daily fresh greens to keep your budgie healthy. Salad greens, dandelion, chickweed, groundsel, spinach, freshly sprouted seeds and seeding grasses are all suitable, or you can offer a slice of apple or carrot wedged in the cage bars. Avoid picking greens which have been exposed to pesticides or pollution, and always wash fruit or vegetables before offering them to your budgie. Never offer tired, wilting greens (or lettuce, which is unsuitable), and remove any uneaten portions before they get to this stage.

21 Clean water must be available at all times

Change your budgie's drinking water twice a day to keep it clean and free of bacteria. Water bowls will need checking and re-filling more often than water bottles. Tap water is acceptable, although if your tap water is heavily chlorinated it should be left to stand in a bowl for a few hours to allow the chlorine to disperse before it is used to re-fill water bottles. If you have doubts about the quality of your tap water, non-carbonated mineral water is a safe (if more expensive) alternative.

Right: This gravity-fed drinking fountain keeps water clean and reduces mess.

SPROUTED SEEDS
To sprout seeds, soak a spoonful of seed mix in a saucer of water, leaving it in a warm place. After 24 hours, rinse and leave to soak for another 24-48 hours, by which time they should have sprouted. Rinse again and discard any mouldy sprouts before serving.

HOW MUCH?
Budgies need to eat little and often. As a rough guide, provide one and a half to two teaspoons of seed per day, re-filling the seed bowl at least once a day and clearing out husks twice daily. Fruit and greens should comprise approximately a quarter of the daily diet.

Right: Grit is essential to enable birds to digest hard seeds.

NITTY GRITTY
Budgies need to eat grit in order to digest their food: seed is swallowed whole, and broken down inside the gizzard with the help of the grit particles. Pet-shops stock suitable fine grit for this purpose. Keep a grit pot in the cage, and ensure it is topped up regularly.

GOLD MEDAL

TIPS

FAT OR FIT?

To check if your budgie is overweight or underweight, look at its chest. If the keel bone running down the centre juts out, he is too thin. If the chest is prominent, with a mid-line indentation over the keel bone, he is too fat. A smooth chest is just right!

Above: A spinach leaf makes a tasty and healthy titbit with which to win your pet's trust.

USING TITBITS

The main purpose of titbits is to make life more interesting for your pet, but they are also very useful to win your pet's trust. A particularly appealing bit of food will make a shy bird more willing to come to hand, and teach him to associate you with treats.

DIET SUPPLEMENTS

A healthy budgie on a balanced diet with regular and varied fresh food is unlikely to need vitamin or mineral supplements to the diet. Specific vitamins or minerals may be needed if the bird is very young, sick or injured, stressed or laying eggs and raising young.

22

Healthy treats can be served daily

These include portions of fruit try apple, grape, guava, kiwi fruit, mango, melon, nectarine, orange, peach, pear, pomegranate, plum, strawberry, or tangerine. Most fruits suitable for human consumption are acceptable, with the exception of avocado, which must be avoided as it can be toxic. Fruit seeds should be removed before serving. Some budgies will enjoy a small amount of protein such as cooked lean meat, cheese, cottage cheese, egg or yoghurt, but be careful to remove uneaten portions promptly, and never over-do dairy products.

Peach

Grapes

Kiwi fruit

Mango

Plum

23

Should budgies eat people food?

An occasional titbit from your plate is unlikely to do any harm. As a general rule, if people can eat it, so can budgies – and if it isn't good for people, it isn't good for budgies either. Since a budgie's intake is so much smaller than a human's, it cannot afford to waste digestive space on junk food. Sticky foods are best avoided, as they can clog the beak, causing distress. A few foods and drinks are actively dangerous to budgies, including fruit seeds, avocado, chocolate, coffee and alcohol.

REATS AND TITBITS

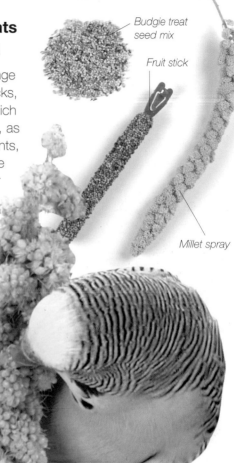

24

Commercial treats can be fattening

Pet-shops stock a range of seed bells, fruit sticks, egg biscuits, etc. which udgies enjoy. However, these are very fattening, as ey are bound together with honey or similar agents, d they are best offered no more often than once a month. Much the same applies to millet sprays, which budgies love. The problem is that millet is fattening, and your bird will already be obtaining a sufficiency of millet from his seed mix. Keep millet sprays for an occasional treat, say fortnightly. Fat budgies are not healthy birds!

Budgie treat seed mix

Fruit stick

Millet spray

Pear

There is a wide range of fruit suitable for gies' consumption. Try different kinds to blish your pet's favourites. Keep ions small to avoid the risk of nach upsets, and remove aten pieces promptly.

ht: Millet sprays vide exercise for t and beaks.

Far right: The short, sturdy beak and strong, muscular tongue are specialist tools for tackling seeds and fruit.

MAKING FRIENDS

Below: Well-meanin
approaches may
frighten a new bird

25

The new arrival

Give your new budgie
time to settle in,
keeping his new
environment as unthreatening as possible.
He won't be able to relax among loud noises, sudden movements or a constant bustle of
activity. Once he starts eating and preening, he is ready to face you. Approach the cage
quietly with fresh food and water, and spend a quarter of an hour or so chatting softly to
him, repeating his new name regularly. Keep this up
every day, and he will soon associate your approach
with food and company, as well as learning his nam

*Below: Gradually
your budgie will
come to view your
finger as a safe
perch.*

Hand-training

26

As soon as your
budgie is com-
fortable in your
presence, start hand-taming. Each day, plac
your hand quietly inside the cage with a little
food on the palm. Keep quite still, talking gen
Eventually (and it may take some time), the bird
will feel confident enough to feed from your hand
Don't rush things! Once he is completely comforta
with hand-feeding, you can move on to
gently stroking his breast and lower
abdomen. The next stage is to move you
finger towards his feet and encourage
him to step on to your finger. Patience is
all-important in building up a relationship
with your new pet.

27 Keep talking

Use your voice constantly to reassure your new pet. He won't understand the words, but you can communicate your good intentions by your tone. Constant and consistent repetition will enable him to learn his name and some simple commands. For example, decide on a fixed word such as 'Home' to use when you want your budgie to return to his cage. Repeat this every time you want him to go back in, and always reward his return, however slow, with a favourite titbit.

EARLY DAYS
During the first few weeks with your budgie, it pays to take extra care to keep the home quiet and peaceful and protect him from shock. Loud music, shouting, door slamming or noisy television programmes should be avoided, as well as sudden shocking changes in light intensity.

DON'T GRAB!
Never grab hold of your bird or try to catch him in flight. If you have to catch him, use a soft cloth or net, not your hand. Hand-taming makes life easier for you and your budgie: hand-tame birds will perch on a finger and let you carry them back.

WING CLIPPING
Clipping a new budgie's wing feathers is sometimes recommended, so that it cannot fly away when you are trying to make friends. However, this is more likely to cause stress (and even distress) to the bird. Patience is a better tool than temporarily disabling your pet.

Left: Budgies are highly social creatures who are much happier living in pairs than singly. It is just as easy to tame two birds as one – budgies appreciate human company as well as that of other birds.

EXERCISE AND RECREATION

28

Budgies need exercise

Allow yourself plenty of time for the first occasion you let your pet out of his cage. Make sure first that doors are shut. Coax the budgie on to your finger, then gently withdraw your hand from the cage, talking to him all the time. He will probably want to fly around the room and explore. It is best to let him take his own time in returning to his cage at first. If you catch him to put him back in, next time it will be harder.

Left: Once your budgie regards your finger as a safe perch, you can start training him to come to your hand when called. Use his favourite titbits to encourage his return, and keep your tone of voice soft, cal and welcomir

Below: Leave the cage door open when your budgie is enjoying free-flying exercise, so t he can pop in if he choos This is his home – don't sh him out of it!

29

The first outing

Once your budgie is hand-tame, he will need daily free-flying time outside the cage in bird-proof room. Block off all escape routes and remove azards such as poisonous plants, potential traps (pots, en drawers, wastepaper baskets), open water vessels ven flower vases) or dangerous substances (alcohol, smetics, ink, lead, adhesives, etc). Windows and irrors should be screened to prevent the bird from flying o the glass. Finally, make sure other family members ow the budgie is out, so that they don't suddenly open e door.

30

Right: A budgie's cage is his home, but he will also enjoy outings into the room.

Below: You can buy a wide variety of toys, mirrors and bells to make your budgie's life more interesting.

Play and toys

dgies are naturally playful and inquisitive. They need the stimulation of toys within the cage, and in the freedom of a room they will find all sorts of things with which to amuse themselves. In fact, you will need to teach

ur bird the word 'No', because he is bound o discover some destructive amusement. discourage him from getting into mischief, u can develop little games to play with him, hiding toys for him to find or teaching him to go to a particular toy on command.

GOLD MEDAL TIPS

USING FOOD
Never feed your budgie outside his cage. He will learn that food is only available in his cage, so that going back is as rewarding as coming out. Leave the cage door open while he is out.

DON'T SCOLD
To a budgie, peeling off wallpaper or plucking a hole in a rug are games like any other. Scolding or punishing such undesirable behaviour will only damage your bird's trust in you. Simply say 'No' and offer a distraction, or pop him back in his cage for a while.

FRESH AIR
In summer, give your bird an outing by popping his cage outdoors for a while. Sunshine is good for him, but never leave him without shelter in direct sun. Many budgies will also enjoy ten minutes or so in light rain taking a natural bath.

CLEANING THE CAGE

31 Daily tasks

Each day, remove old food and droppings. Change the sand sheet or, if you have chosen sand or gravel for a floor covering, remove soiled patches with a spoon and replace with fresh material. Soiled perches may also need cleaning. Every morning, food bowls should be emptied out, washed in hot water and thoroughly dried before re-filling. Refill the water bottle, and don't forget to clear husks from the food bowl twice a day.

Right: Hygiene matters! In the wild, birds can fly away from the mess they make. A caged bird is dependent on you to keep his home clear and clean.

32 Weekly tasks

Once a week, clean the entire cage and all its contents thoroughly, using hot water or suitably diluted pet-safe disinfectant. Never use household detergents, which are dangerous to birds. Wash and brush down the bars, scrub perches and toys, and replace chewed branches where necessary. Don't forget to replenish the gr pot. Hand-tame pets can be le loose in the room during cleaning sessions, but you may prefer to pop your pet into a spare cage while you work.

33 Cleaning kit

is not advisable to clean your
rd's cage with the same
quipment used for the family
shes, so keep a separate
rge bowl for washing food
owls, toys, etc. You will need
scraper, a small,
ard scrubbing
rush, and a
uitable disinfectant. A holding
age may be useful to house
our bird while you work. If he
to fly free during cleaning,
eep a net or soft cloth to
and to catch him in any
mergency.

*Right: Birds need clean
surroundings so they can
keep their feathers in clean
and healthy condition.*

*Above: Birds
may be messy in
their cages, but
they are scrupulous
about personal
hygiene. Feathers
need constant
grooming with beak
and claws to keep
them clean, supple,
waterproofed and
in top condition.*

Disinfectants 34

ven a cage which looks clean
ill need periodical disinfecting,
as it soon accumulates dirt,
dust, traces of food and droppings and feather dust,
which form a breeding ground for bacteria. Disinfectants
only work on a surface which has been scrubbed clean
first. Any organic material, such as caked droppings,
emaining on the surface will prevent the disinfectant from
taking effect. After disinfecting the cage, always give it
a thorough rinse in fresh water and make sure it is
completely dry before returning the occupant.

GOLD MEDAL TIPS

DIAGNOSTIC DROPPINGS

*When cleaning out your budgie,
check that his droppings are
normal. Loose, watery droppings
or faeces containing blood or
undigested seed are warning
signs. Altering your bird's diet and
ensuring that he is not stressed
may solve the problem, but if it
persists seek veterinary advice.*

*Above: Check the sand sheet
for unhealthy-looking droppings,
a sign of illness which should
never be ignored.*

SAFETY CHECKS

*When cleaning the cage, take
the opportunity to check for
damage and danger areas.
Keep an eye out for rust and any
sharp edges or splintery perches
which could cause injury, and
check that the door and its
catches are secure.*

OUTSIDE THE CAGE

*Budgies can't be house-trained,
so occasional droppings in the
room are unavoidable when your
pet enjoys his free-flying exercise
in the room. Most mess will
occur beneath his favourite
perches, so spread paper over
this area before you let him out.*

FEATHERS, FEE[T]

Budgies spend several hours a day preening

They take great care of their plumage, cleaning and smoothing each feather with their beaks, for a bird with dirty, bent feathers cannot fly. At the same time they protect and waterproof the feathers by spreading oil over them from an oil gland situated on the lower back. You can help with feather maintenance by giving your budgie the opportunity to take regular baths, which keep the feathers clean and also stimulate preening.

Moulting is natural

Like all birds, budgies periodically shed their feathers and grow new ones.
This takes some time – the smallest feather[s] take about three weeks to re-grow, while th[e] long tail feathers take some two months.

Above: The beak is a budgie's main grooming tool for feather care.

During the moult, your pet needs a warm, quiet environment and nutritious food that is rich in vitamins and minerals to help him grow strong replacement feathers. If he is under-nourished at this stage, the new feathers may be stunted and weak.

Above: Self-grooming is quite a gymnastic exercise!

AND BEAKS

37

Claw care

A budgie's claws, like our fingernails, grow slowly but continually. Normally they are kept down to a comfortable

Above: A budgie's feet are hand-like gripping tools, so claws need to be well-maintained.

length by use. However, caged birds (especially older rds and those deprived of varied perches to exercise the eet) may suffer from over-grown claws, making it hard for them to perch or climb. Long claws must be clipped, a sk best left to the vet unless you have some experience, s it is easy to cut through the blood vessels in the claw.

Beaks can be bothersome too

38

budgie's beak is an ssential tool, used to rack open seeds, preen feathers and sist in climbing. Like his claws, it grows hroughout his lifetime and is kept in trim y whetting. Occasionally, a bird's beak usually the upper bill, but sometimes oth upper and lower) may become overgrown, making it hard for the bird to eat. This is commoner in older birds. Beak-trimming is a sk for the vet, and an affected bird may need regular treatments.

Left: The beak is a 'third hand' to grip and hold objects.

GOLD MEDAL TIPS

39

Budgies watch out for danger

They have good colour vision and can take in details nearly ten times faster than we can. They have a wider field of vision than we do, with a better rear view (but poorer front view), designed to spot predators approaching. Even tame budgies react to anything that looks like a predator, so they fear hands swooping down on them from above or behind, and should be approached from in front and below.

NOT NIPPING

Budgies use their beaks to investigate things. If your pet leans towards you with his beak, don't snatch your hand away thinking that he is going to bite. He is probably just checking that your finger is a safe perch.

Above: Offering regurgitated food is a signal of strong affection in budgie society.

AFFECTIONATE NATURE

Budgies are sociable creatures who show affection by preening each other. They will even preen a human owner, nibbling hair or eyelashes. A loving budgie may regurgitate food for his owner, just as he would to his mate!

SLEEP IS VITAL

Budgies need 10-12 hours of sleep a night. Lack of sleep will make your pet irritable or even ill – just like us. You may need to cover your pet's cage in the evening to make sure he has enough hours of darkness.

Right: A cage cover creates an artificial night to extend your budgie's bedtime hours.

Budgies are naturally chatty

40

They are social birds which chatter among themselves, and they enjoy human conversation. They often also enjoy household sounds including human speech. This makes it possible to teach budgies to talk. Individuals vary: some never talk, while others can acquire a large vocabulary. You can encourage your pet to talk by repeating a phrase over and over again in exactly the same way. Keep training sessions short, frequent and regular for best results.

UNDERSTANDING YOUR BUDGIE

ow to hold your budgie

or any but the tamest birds, being held in a hand is a
ressful experience. However, on occasion you may
eed to hold your pet. Bring your hand down over
s back and fold your fingers
ound him, holding his wings
ose to his body, with your
dex and middle finger on each
de of his head and your other
gers encircling his abdomen.
sk your local pet-shop staff to
emonstrate the technique if you
e in any doubt.

Climbing is as natural to a budgie as flying

42

Like all members of the parrot family, they
have specially adapted feet to help them
grip and climb. Generally, they like to cover
short distances by climbing, and longer
distances by flying. Cagebirds need the
stimulus of other birds to encourage them
to take flying exercise, and a single budgie
may not use his wings enough to keep
fit. Two budgies are more likely to stay
healthy and active than a singleton.

*Left: Budgies' feet and beaks are designed as climbing
aids appropriate for a life in the tree-tops, and will be
used in the same way in a cage, where the bars
provide a convenient climbing frame for exercise.*

HEALT

Take time to make a daily health check

This enables you to spot any symptoms at an early stage Watch out for any change in your pet's behaviour. A sick budgie is usually lethargic and will sit huddled up in a corner of the cage. Loss of appetite and ruffled, neglecte feathers should never be ignored. Other warning signs to take seriously include a sore or dirty vent, noisy breathin runny nostrils, lameness, abnormal droppings and crusted face, legs or feet.

Above:
Check
droppings for
any abnormality.

LUMPS AND BUMPS

Lumps and swellings should always be seen by a vet, as they may require surgery. Budgies are sadly prone to growths and tumours, but lumps may also be caused by abscesses, feather cysts or hernias, which can often be treated successfully.

LEG RINGS

Budgies bred by exhibitors often have a metal ring on one leg with an identifying number. If your budgie has a ring, check it regularly in case it grows too tight, catches on something or rubs the leg, in which case your vet will have to cut the ring off.

Above: Leg rings usually cause no problems, but need checking.

DISTINCTIVE DROPPINGS

A change in the appearance of your bird's droppings is an obvious sign that something is wrong. Mild diarrhoea is often caused by digestive problems and may be resolved by cutting out green food, but severe cases call for veterinary treatment.

Ailing birds need prompt action

A sick bird's condition can deteriorate surprisingly quickly, so it is vital to take your budgie to the vet at the first sign of illness. Many budgie diseases have confusingly similar symptoms, so a professional diagnosis is important. In terms of first aid until you can get to the vet, warmth and quiet are the most important elements. Subdued lighting (not complete darkness) will also help by calming the invalid and encouraging him to rest.

ND AILMENTS

Lice, mites and parasites

A number of unpleasant conditions are caused by parasites. Feather lice, red mites and other parasites can cause loss or damage to feathers. Crusty, scaly growths on beaks or legs are the result of infestation by another kind of mite. Obtain treatment from the vet, and also disinfect the cage and all its contents to prevent a currence of infection. If you have more than one bird, you must treat all of them even if only one seems affected.

Right: 'Scaly face', caused by mite infestation, needs prompt treatment to prevent serious beak deformities.

low: A small carrying x is the safest way transport your et to the vet.

Respiratory problems

Noisy and laboured breathing, perhaps with a bubbly discharge from the nostrils, needs treatment with antibiotics. If you cannot get to the vet straight away, place the bird in a ventilated box and keep it warm. A gently steaming kettle nearby may help the invalid to breathe more easily. Some respiratory illnesses of birds can be transmitted to humans, so if you start having breathing problems yourself, tell your doctor that you have a pet bird in the house.

Left: Transparent carrying boxes should be covered with a cloth to make travel less alarming.

BREEDING ADVICE

Below: A nest-box made specifically for budgies is designed to imitate the cavity in a hollow tree which would be the bird's first choice in the wild.

Sliding door

Plywood nest-box

Entrance hole

Perch

Sliding perspex inspection window

Timber concave (where eggs are laid)

Think before you breed

Most pet owners will be content to enjoy the company of their budgie without breeding from them. If you do decide to breed from your pets you will need time and commitmer suitable accommodation for more birds, and a source of good home for the babies.

Only breed from tame, healthy birds. There are already far more budgies being bred than there are good homes for them, so don't add to the numbers of unwanted pets.

Budgies don't build nest

In the wild, they lay their eggs in holes in trees or rocks; in captivity, they need a specia nest-box. They can lay two or three clutches a year of five or six eggs at a time laid on alternate days. These hatch at two-day intervals after eighteen days' incubation to yield naked, helpless youngsters. Both parents feed the young, who develop quickly and are ready to leave the nest at six weeks.

are of breeding stock

...dgies can breed at two ...onths old, but should not be ...owed to do so until they are ten ...onths. Aviary birds will choose ...eir own mates. If you have just one pair, they will need ...breeding cage with a nest-box designed for budgies. ...e hen will need special food while laying eggs and ...aring young. Once her ...ung leave the nest, she ...l be ready to lay again. ...o broods in a row is ...ough: after this, remove ...e nest-box to ...ow her a ...st.

49

Young chicks quickly develop feathers.

NEST-BOXES
Budgies need nest-boxes measuring 25cm by 15cm by 15 cm (10in by 6in by 6in), with a small entrance hole with perch below. Inside the box they need a block with a hollow to accommodate the eggs. The top of the box should ideally hinge up for inspection and easy cleaning.

HYGIENE AND HEALTH
Nestlings need checking regularly to make sure no dirt is stuck to their toes or inside their beaks, which can cause deformities. Soak dirty feet in lukewarm water to loosen the dirt before picking it off carefully. Dirty beaks can be cleaned gently with a toothpick.

aising the young

50

...by budgies are fragile and ...ould not be handled before ...ey are two weeks old. ...ereafter, you will need to ...ove them to clean the nest-box, and to check their ...alth. Special rearing food with extra protein is needed ...help them grow. The youngsters need separating from ...eir parents once they leave the nest-box, to stop them ...sturbing the next clutch. Males and females should be ...parated at twelve weeks.

EGG PROBLEMS
If a hen is straining unsuccessfully to lay an egg which has become stuck ('egg binding'), she needs veterinary assistance. An unmated female may lay infertile eggs, which are best left for her to incubate uselessly – removing them will only encourage her to lay more and exhaust herself.

Further Information

Recommended Books

Birmelin, Immanuel, *Budgerigars, A Complete Pet Owner's Manual* (Barrons, 1998)

Barnes, Julia, *101 Facts about Budgerigars* (Ringpress Books, 2002)

Harper, Don, *Caring for Your Pet: Budgies* (Interpet Publishing, 1999)

Moizer, Stan and Barbara, *Pet Owner's Guide to the Budgerigar* (Ringpress Books, 1997)

Page, Gill, *Getting To Know Your Budgie* (Interpet Publishing, 2001)

Rach, Julie, *An Owner's Guide to a Happy, Healthy Pet: The Budgie* (Howell Book House, 199

Thompson, Eric, *How to Care for Your Budgerigar* (Kingdom Books, 2001)

Recommended Websites

http://www.aviarybirds.com/educational.htm
http://www.budgerigars.co.uk/index.html
http://www.geocities.com/RainForest/3298
http://www.petnet.com.au/bird/budgerigar.html

Acknowledgements

The author and publisher would like to offer sincere thanks to Jackie Wilson of Rolf C. Hagen (UK) Ltd who supplied equipment for photography in this book. Thanks also go to models Bronwyn and Stephanie McGuire, Victoria and Louise Etheridge and Danielle Taylor, to Hassocks Pet Centre, West Sussex for providing a nest-box for photography, and to Peter Dean and Andrea Margrie at Interpet Ltd for their help with photographic props.

Picture Credits

The majority of the photographs reproduced were taken by Neil Sutherland specifically for this book and are the copyright of Interpet Publishing. All other pictures are also the copyright of Interpet Publishing with the exception of the following:
Frank Lane Picture Agency: pages 5 top (David Hosking), 7 centre (Foto Natura Stock/ J. & P. Wegner), 7 lower (A.R. Hamblin), 8 upper (A.R. Hamblin), 29 upper right (A.R. Hamblin), 31 (H.V. Lacey).
RSPCA Photolibrary: page 20 bottom (Angela Hampton).